1 Introduction

When firms evaluate whether their cost of entering into a new market can be recouped, they must consider both the entry decisions of their rivals and the nature of post-entry competition. The firms' entry decisions affect not only their own expected profits, but also the expected profits of other market participants. Consequently, understanding how firms' entry behavior responds to different market conditions is quite important to every player in the market. For example, the firms' customers and suppliers can maximize their profits by optimally selecting from how many of the firms to solicit bids when they let procurement contracts, while antitrust agencies can improve social welfare by evaluating reductions in or restrictions on the number of potential entrants.

Two recent papers examine simultaneous and costly entry decisions by homogeneous product Bertrand competitors with identical entry costs. The key difference between Elberfeld and Wolfstetter [1999] (hereafter EW) and Lang and Rosenthal [1991] (hereafter LR) is that in the EW model the firms learn the identity of all entrants before they make their pricing decisions.[1] In contrast, in the LR model the firms do not learn the number or identity of other entrants before they make their pricing decisions.[2] Despite this important distinction, the two models' results are surprisingly similar. EW find that adding more identical potential entrants decreases expected total welfare, while LR find that adding more identical potential entrants increases the expected price.[3] Both results contradict the conventional wisdom that the degree of competition increases in the number of potential entrants. The reasoning underlying both results is that an increase in the number of potential entrants reduces the likelihood that any particular firm enters. In equilibrium, the reduction in the original firms' entry likelihood is sufficiently great that it outweighs the effect of the new potential entrant's probability of entry. Moreover, the lower likelihood of rivals' entry leads to on average less aggressive price-setting by firms that do enter.

If these models are to be considered accurate representations of the entry process, then the robustness of their counterintuitive results must be tested. In this paper I extend the EW and LR models by introducing the plausible assumption that the potential entrants have different entry

[1]Levin and Smith [1994] examine the same problem in an auction context, in which firms see who has entered, but are uninformed about rivals' production costs. Their main results are qualitatively the same as those presented in EW. I use the more recent paper as a starting point because its model is more closely related to the LR model.

[2]In a related paper, Janssen and Rasmusen [1999] analyze the pricing decisions of firms that have an equal and exogenously specified likelihood of entering the market. Assuming that the firms do not learn the number or identity of other entrants before they make their pricing decisions, the authors characterize post-entry prices and profits. Though Janssen and Rasmusen [1999] exogenously specify the firms' entry probabilities, those probabilities can be determined endogenously by imposing entry costs, as is done in LR.

[3]Sharkey and Sibley [1993] find the same result in an extension of the LR model that permits certain nonlinear pricing schemes, in addition to the uniform prices used by LR.

costs. These differences might arise from scale or scope effects in the firms' lines of business, or from differences in the firms' outside opportunities. I find that the central results in both models depend critically on the symmetry assumption.

In the observed entry setting, expected total welfare can increase following the introduction of a potential entrant, reversing the main result in EW. Welfare increases when the introduction of a sufficiently low cost potential entrant induces one or more existing high cost potential entrants to become inactive, in the sense that they choose to enter with probability zero. However, it is the case that expected total welfare falls with an increase in the number of firms entering with positive probability, which follows from the logic described previously.

In the unobserved entry setting, the equilibrium outcome generally does not involve all firms entering with positive probability. For example, if all firms' entry costs differ, then the unique equilibrium involves strictly positive entry probabilities only for the two firms with the lowest and second lowest entry costs. If multiple firms all have the lowest entry cost, then in equilibrium only those firms enter with positive probability. In contrast, in the symmetric setting the symmetric equilibrium involves all firms entering with the same probability. Thus, the symmetric model is a very special case of the more general model, and introducing arbitrarily small differences in firms' entry costs yields vastly different predictions about entry and pricing. Moreover, the expected price typically decreases or remains unchanged following the introduction of a potential entrant in the asymmetric model, in contrast to the unambiguous price increase found in the symmetric setting.

The essential feature of my findings is that simply increasing the number of potential entrants does not dampen competition. Instead, competition decreases if the introduction of a potential entrant increases the number of firms that enter with positive probability. However, if a new potential entrant has a sufficiently low entry cost, then one or more previously active firms will now enter with probability zero. In this instance,the introduction of a new potential entrant increases competition. This finding is obscured in the symmetric models, because a new potential entrant always can be accommodated without requiring a previously active firm to become inactive.

Section 2 examines the equilibria of the observed entry setting, and compares the symmetric and asymmetric outcomes. Section 3 does the same for the unobserved entry setting, while Section 4 briefly concludes. An Appendix contains all proofs.

2 Bertrand Competition with Observed Entry

Consider a two-stage entry and pricing game with $N' \geq 2$ firms producing perfect substitutes for a consumer with demand $D(p)$ for the good. The firms' marginal production cost is normalized to zero, and the monopoly price, p_m, uniquely maximizes $pD(p)$, with $\pi_m \equiv p_m D(p_m)$. In the first stage of the game, the firms simultaneously decide whether to enter the market. If firm i enters, then it pays an entry cost $E_i \geq 0$. If firm i does not enter, then it pays nothing and earns zero profit. Assume $E_i < \pi_m$ for all i, as a firm with an entry cost exceeding π_m will not enter, and so has no effect on the analysis. I refer to the N' firms as **potential entrants**. In the second stage of the game, each entrant learns the number and identity of all other entrants. Each entrant then simultaneously selects the price it offers to the buyer. The buyer purchases $D(p)$ units from the firm offering the lowest price at the price that firm offered, with ties among sellers resolved by a fair lottery.

Due to the nature of the post-entry price competition, if two or more firms enter the market, then at least two of them set a price of zero. This competitive outcome occurs in all Nash equilibria of the one-shot Bertrand competition in the second stage of the game. If only one firm enters, then that firm sets a price of p_m and earns π_m. Firms are risk neutral, so firm i's profit if it wins with price p_i is $p_i D(p_i) - E_i$. If the monopoly price of p_m is set, then consumer surplus is CS_m. If the competitive price of zero is set, then consumer surplus is CS_c, with $CS_c > CS_m$.

This game has two types of equilibria. In the first type, firm $i \in \{1, ..., N'\}$ enters with probability one and charges p_m, while all other firms stay out. There are N' of these equilibria. In the second type, $k > 1$ firms enter with positive probability and the remaining firms stay out. To facilitate comparison with EW's results from their symmetric model, I define a **maximal Nash equilibrium** to be a Nash equilibrium of the second type consisting of the largest number of firms, which may or may not be the entire set of N' firms.[4] I restrict attention to maximal Nash equilibria, because EW focus on the Nash equilibrium in which each of the N' identical firms enters with the same probability. That equilibrium is their model's unique maximal Nash equilibrium.

This two-stage game is solved through backward induction. Let the maximal Nash equilibrium include exactly N of the N' firms. I refer to the N firms as **active** potential entrants, and the $N' - N$ firms not in the maximal Nash equilibrium as **inactive** potential entrants. Order the active firms so that $E_1 \leq E_2 \leq \cdots \leq E_N$.[5] In stage two, suppose that each firm k has entered with probability α_k^o, where "o" denotes the observed entry game. Let $\boldsymbol{\alpha}^o = \{\alpha_1^o, ..., \alpha_N^o\}$, and let $\mathbf{E} = \{E_1, E_2, ..., E_N\}$. Because firm i sets a price of p_m if it is the only entrant, and sets a price of

[4]Note that there may exist several maximal Nash equilibria.

[5]Note that I am not requring the N firms to be those with the lowest entry costs. The results to follow hold for any maximal Nash equilibrium.

zero otherwise, its expected profit from entry, gross of entry costs, is

$$\pi_i^o(\boldsymbol{\alpha}^o, \pi_m) = \left(\prod_{k \neq i} (1 - \alpha_k^o)\right) \pi_m.$$

For firm i to be willing to mix between the pure actions of entering and not entering, the payoffs from these two actions must be identical. Thus, in equilibrium firm i's expected profit, net of entry costs, must equal zero, the payoff from not entering. That is, for each firm i,

$$\left(\prod_{k \neq i} (1 - \alpha_k^o)\right) \pi_m = E_i.$$

From the requirements for each of the N firms, one can determine the equilibrium values of the entry probabilities in terms of the entry costs, $\mathbf{E}$, and the monopoly profit, π_m. Denote the vector of equilibrium entry probabilities by $\boldsymbol{\alpha}^o(\mathbf{E}, \pi_m)$.

The buyer's surplus depends on how many firms enter. The probability that zero firms enter, which EW refer to as market breakdown (b), is

$$\rho_b(\boldsymbol{\alpha}^o) = \prod_{i=1}^{N} (1 - \alpha_i^o).$$

The probability that only one firm enters, which EW refer to as monopoly (m), is

$$\rho_m(\boldsymbol{\alpha}^o) = \sum_{i=1}^{N} \alpha_i^o \left(\prod_{k \neq i} (1 - \alpha_k^o)\right),$$

where the term in the summation is the probability that firm i is the only firm that enters. Finally, the probability that two or more firms enter, which EW refer to as competition (c), is

$$\rho_c(\boldsymbol{\alpha}^o) = 1 - \rho_b(\boldsymbol{\alpha}^o) - \rho_m(\boldsymbol{\alpha}^o).$$

Expected consumer surplus is

$$CS^o(\boldsymbol{\alpha}^o) = \rho_m(\boldsymbol{\alpha}^o)\, CS_m + \rho_c(\boldsymbol{\alpha}^o)\, CS_c,$$

and expected total welfare is the sum of expected consumer and producer surplus. Hence,

$$W^o(\boldsymbol{\alpha}^o, \mathbf{E}, \pi_m) = CS^o(\boldsymbol{\alpha}^o) + \sum_{i=1}^{N} \alpha_i^o \left[\pi_i^o(\boldsymbol{\alpha}^o, \pi_m) - E_i\right].$$

As $\pi_i^o(\boldsymbol{\alpha}^o, \pi_m) = E_i$ in equilibrium, expected total welfare in equilibrium is determined entirely by expected consumer surplus.

Lemma 1 *Suppose that all firms have strictly positive entry costs, and that* $E_1 \geq \left(\frac{1}{\pi_m}\prod_{k=1}^{N} E_k\right)^{\frac{1}{N-1}}$. *There exists a Nash equilibrium in which each of the N firms enters the market with non-negative probability. Firm i enters with probability*

$$\alpha_i^o(\mathbf{E}, \pi_m) = 1 - \frac{\left(\frac{1}{\pi_m}\prod_{k=1}^{N} E_k\right)^{\frac{1}{N-1}}}{E_i}.$$

The probability of market breakdown is

$$\rho_b(\boldsymbol{\alpha}^o) = \left(\frac{1}{\pi_m}\right)^{\frac{N}{N-1}} \left(\prod_{k=1}^{N} E_k\right)^{\frac{1}{N-1}},$$

while the probability of competition is

$$\rho_c(\boldsymbol{\alpha}^o) = 1 + (N-1)\left(\frac{1}{\pi_m}\right)^{\frac{N}{N-1}} \left(\prod_{k=1}^{N} E_k\right)^{\frac{1}{N-1}} - \frac{1}{\pi_m}\left(\sum_{k=1}^{N} E_k\right).$$

Therefore, expected total welfare is

$$\begin{aligned} W^o(\boldsymbol{\alpha}^o, \mathbf{E}, \pi_m) = {} & \left[\frac{1}{\pi_m}\left(\sum_{k=1}^{N} E_k\right) - N\left(\frac{1}{\pi_m}\right)^{\frac{N}{N-1}} \left(\prod_{k=1}^{N} E_k\right)^{\frac{1}{N-1}}\right] CS_m + \\ & \left[1 + (N-1)\left(\frac{1}{\pi_m}\right)^{\frac{N}{N-1}} \left(\prod_{k=1}^{N} E_k\right)^{\frac{1}{N-1}} - \frac{1}{\pi_m}\left(\sum_{k=1}^{N} E_k\right)\right] CS_c. \end{aligned}$$

The condition on E_1 in Lemma 1 ensures that all N firms enter with non-negative probability. If the condition did not hold, then there would be an internal inconsistency, as the solution would imply that firm 1's entry probability is *negative*, which cannot occur. In such an instance, if firm 1's entry probability were constrained to be zero and if all other firms adjusted their entry probabilities accordingly, then one can show that firm 1 would have a strictly positive payoff from entry, net of its entry costs. Hence, firm 1 would enter with probability one, which would unravel the purported equilibrium and would imply that firm 1 and at most $N-2$ other firms are in the maximal Nash equilibrium.

Corollary 1 *All else equal, a firm's entry probability strictly increases as its entry cost increases if it has at least two rivals, and does not change otherwise. In contrast, a firm's entry probability strictly decreases as a rival's entry cost increases. A firm with a higher entry cost is strictly more likely to enter than is a firm with a lower entry cost. Moreover, the probability of market breakdown strictly increases, and total welfare strictly decreases, as any firm's entry cost increases. Formally,*

(1) $\frac{d\alpha_i^o(\mathbf{E},\pi_m)}{dE_i} > (=)0$ *when* $N > (=)2$, *for all* i.

(2) $\frac{d\alpha_i^o(\mathbf{E},\pi_m)}{dE_j} < 0$, *for* $j \neq i$.

(3) $E_i > E_j \Rightarrow \alpha_i^o(\mathbf{E},\pi_m) > \alpha_j^o(\mathbf{E},\pi_m)$

(4) $\frac{d\rho_b(\alpha^o)}{dE_i} > 0$, *for all* i.

(5) $\frac{dW^o(\alpha^o,\mathbf{E},\pi_m)}{dE_i} < 0$, *for all* i.

Parts (1) and (2) can be explained by noting that when firm i's entry cost increases, the remaining firms must enter less frequently in order for firm i to remain indifferent between entering and not entering. In order to keep any other firm k indifferent between entering and not entering, firm i must enter more frequently to make up for the reduction in the frequency of entry of firms other than i and k.[6] Part (4) follows because the decrease in firm i's probability of not entering just offsets the increase in the probability of not entering by all firms other than i and k, and because of the increase in firm k's probability of not entering. Part (3) follows directly from the mixed strategy nature of the equilibrium. A firm with a low entry cost must expect to receive lower profit, gross of entry costs, than does a firm with a higher entry cost. The difference in the two firms' expected gross profits is driven by the difference in the probabilities that each of them does not enter. Hence, the firm with a lower entry cost must be less likely to enter than the firm with a higher entry cost. Finally, Part (5) follows because $CS_c > CS_m$ and because the decrease in the probability of competition outweighs any possible increase in the probability of monopoly.

EW's results are obtained from Lemma 1 by assuming that the entry costs are identical across firms. The maximal Nash equilibrium includes all N' firms.

[6]Note that the latter increase is unnecessary if there exist only two firms, which explains the $N = 2$ condition in Part (1).

Result 1 (EW) *Suppose that all firms have the same entry cost $E > 0$. In the maximal Nash equilibrium, all firms enter with probability*

$$\alpha^o(\mathbf{E}, \pi_m) = 1 - \left(\frac{E}{\pi_m}\right)^{\frac{1}{N'-1}}.$$

The probability of market breakdown is

$$\rho_b(\boldsymbol{\alpha}^o) = \left(\frac{E}{\pi_m}\right)^{\frac{N'}{N'-1}},$$

while the probability of competition is

$$\rho_c(\boldsymbol{\alpha}^o) = 1 + (N'-1)\left(\frac{E}{\pi_m}\right)^{\frac{N'}{N'-1}} - \frac{N'E}{\pi_m}.$$

Therefore, expected total welfare is

$$W^o(\boldsymbol{\alpha}^o, \mathbf{E}, \pi_m) = \left[\frac{N'E}{\pi_m} - N'\left(\frac{E}{\pi_m}\right)^{\frac{N'}{N'-1}}\right] CS_m + \left[1 + (N'-1)\left(\frac{E}{\pi_m}\right)^{\frac{N'}{N'-1}} - \frac{N'E}{\pi_m}\right] CS_c.$$

The probability of market breakdown strictly increases, and expected total welfare strictly decreases, as the number of firms increases.

The next two propositions follow directly from Lemma 1. To aid the discussion to follow, I introduce the following definition. Suppose that the original maximal Nash equilibrium consists of N firms, and that a new potential entrant is introduced, with entry cost E_e. It is either the case that the new maximal Nash equilibrium consists of $N+1$ firms, or that the new maximal Nash equilibrium consists of N firms or less. The latter occurs if the solution with $N+1$ firms violates the condition on E_1 in Lemma 1 (or the corresponding condition on E_e, if $E_e < E_1$). I say that the introduction of a potential entrant **induces exit** if and only if the new maximal Nash equilibrium consists of N firms or less and the new potential entrant's entry cost is strictly less than E_N. I use this definition to capture the idea that the introduction of the new firm induces one of the firms in the original maximal Nash equilibrium to become inactive, in the sense that it enters with probability zero. For example, suppose that initially there were three potential entrants in the maximal Nash equilibrium, with $\pi_m = 10$, $E_1 = 2$, $E_2 = 3$, and $E_3 = 4$. If a fourth potential entrant is introduced with $E_e = 3.5$, then any new maximal Nash equilibria consist of only three firms.

As the new potential entrant's entry cost is less than firm 3's entry cost, it seems most reasonable to focus attention on the new maximal Nash equilibrium in which firm 3 becomes inactive. In contrast, it seems less reasonable to consider an equilibrium in which firm 2 does not enter, though one could construct such an equilibrium. Similarly, if $E_e = 4.5$, then it seems unreasonable to consider equilibria in which any of the original firms become inactive.[7]

With the preceding definition and with the characterization in Lemma 1, it is straightforward to prove the following results.

Proposition 1 *The introduction of a potential entrant strictly decreases the probability of market breakdown if and only if it induces exit.*

The finding that entry can decrease the probability of market breakdown reverses the first of two main results in EW. The more important finding is how the introduction of a potential entrant relates to total welfare.

Proposition 2 *The introduction of a potential entrant strictly increases expected total welfare if and only if it induces exit.*

By reversing the second main result in EW, Proposition 2 shows that the conclusion that additional potential entry reduces total welfare is not robust to the consideration of potential entrants whose entry costs differ. More importantly, Proposition 2 illustrates fundamentally how the introduction of a potential entrant affects total welfare in the observed entry setting, the reasons for which are masked in the symmetric model. Proposition 1 follows from a similar argument.

If the introduction of a potential entrant increases the number of active potential entrants, even if the new firm has a low entry cost, then total welfare strictly decreases. To see why this occurs, imagine E_e is such that the new potential entrant enters with probability zero.[8] In this instance the number of firms in the maximal Nash equilibrium has increased by one, but total welfare remains unchanged. As E_e increases, application of the Corollary shows that total welfare falls. Thus, it is the case that an increase in the number of active potential entrants, in the sense of an increase in the number of firms in the maximal Nash equilibrium, reduces total welfare. Therefore, if $N > 2$

[7] One might take a more agnostic view about equilibrium selection, and instead limit attention to situations in which the condition on E_e in Lemma 1 is violated, so that some firm other than the new potential entrant *must* become inactive. Using that criterion, all of the results to follow still hold, though their necessary conditions apply less frequently.

[8] E_e cannot be any lower, else the new maximal Nash equilibrium will not contain all N original firms.

firms are in the maximal Nash equilibrium, then total welfare always is increased by reducing the number of active potential entrants to 2.

If the introduction of a potential entrant induces exit, then that is equivalent to holding the number of active firms constant and reducing one firm's entry cost. Part (2) of the Corollary shows that the remaining original firms are more likely to enter than they were before the introduction. This increase outweighs the reduction in the new firm's probability of entry, relative to the entry probability of the firm whose exit was induced, as is shown by applying Part (5) of the Corollary. Consequently, expected total welfare strictly increases.

In the general setting in which costs differ, the proof of Proposition 2 shows why expected total welfare falls as the number of active potential entrants increases. In the symmetric model, the introduction of a new potential entrant always can be accommodated without inducing exit. Consequently, expected total welfare strictly decreases in the number of potential entrants.

3 Bertrand Competition with Unobserved Entry

Consider a two-stage entry and pricing game identical to the one presented in Section 2, with the exception that entrants do not learn the number or identity of any other entrants before each simultaneously selects the price it offers to the buyer. This game is identical to one variant studied by LR, with a slight modification that permits more general demand functions than the inelastic demand structure that they imposed. As will be evident, their results in the symmetric setting continue to hold with more general assumptions about demand.

This two-stage game is solved through backward induction. In stage two, suppose each firm k has entered with probability α_k^u, where "u" denotes the unobserved entry game. Let $\boldsymbol{\alpha}^u = \{\alpha_1^u, ..., \alpha_{N'}^u\}$. Because entry is unobserved, the post-entry competition does not have the all-or-nothing character seen in the observed entry setting. Instead, entrants set their prices using mixed strategies. This pricing game is very similar to a first-price auction in which firms' costs either are zero or exceed p_m.[9] For technical reasons, assume that $pD(p)$ is strictly increasing for $p < p_m$.[10]

Lemma 2 *Suppose that all firms have different entry costs. There exists a unique Nash equilibrium in which firm 1 enters with probability one and firm 2 enters with probability*

$$\alpha_2^u(\mathbf{E}, \pi_m) = 1 - \frac{E_2}{\pi_m}.$$

[9]See Thomas [1998] for a related model.

[10]See Janssen and Rasmusen [1999] for details on this assumption, which is necessary to ensure that the equilibrium mixed strategy price-setting distributions are strictly increasing in the price.

All other firms stay out. Upon entering, firms 1 and 2 set their prices according to the mixed strategy distributions

$$F_1(p) = \begin{cases} 1 - \frac{E_2}{pD(p)} & \text{for } p \in [\underline{p}, p_m) \\ 1 & \text{for } p = p_m \end{cases}$$

and

$$F_2(p) = \frac{1}{1 - \frac{E_2}{\pi_m}} \left[1 - \frac{E_2}{pD(p)} \right] \text{ for } p \in [\underline{p}, p_m],$$

respectively. Firm 1's expected profit, net of entry costs, is $E_2 - E_1 > 0$. *Firm 2's expected profit, net of entry costs, is zero.*

Firm 1's expected profit is positive in this setting, in contrast to the unobserved entry setting with identical entry costs across firms or to the observed entry setting. The reason that only the two firms with the lowest entry costs enter with positive probability is that, upon entering, each firm expects to earn the same profit, gross of entry costs. If firm 3 also entered with positive probability, then its expected profit upon entering must be no less than E_3. If that is the case, then both firms 1 and 2 expect to earn positive profits, net of entry costs. With that expectation, both firm 1 and firm 2 would enter with probability one, in which case their expected profit upon entering would be zero, a contradiction.

If multiple firms have the lowest entry cost, then the equilibrium is quite different.

Lemma 3 *Suppose that the first* $k > 1$ *firms have identical entry cost* $E > 0$, *and that the remaining* $N' - k$ *firms have strictly higher entry costs. There exists a symmetric maximal Nash equilibrium in which each of the first* k *firms enters with probability*

$$\alpha^u(\mathbf{E}, \pi_m) = 1 - \left(\frac{E}{\pi_m} \right)^{\frac{1}{k-1}},$$

while the remaining firms stay out. Upon entering, the firms set their prices according to the mixed strategy distribution

$$F(p) = \frac{1}{1 - \left(\frac{E}{\pi_m} \right)^{\frac{1}{k-1}}} \left[1 - \left(\frac{E}{pD(p)} \right)^{\frac{1}{k-1}} \right] \text{ for } p \in [\underline{p}, p_m].$$

Each firm's expected profit, net of entry costs, is zero.

A result similar to Lemmas 2 and 3 obtains if firm 1 has the lowest entry cost and firms 2 through

k have the second lowest.

As noted earlier, LR's Theorem 1 can be extended to demand functions other than the inelastic demand curve they consider. This is a consequence of Lemma 3, with $k = N'$.

Result 2 (LR) *Suppose that all firms have identical entry cost $E > 0$. In the maximal Nash equilibrium, each firm enters with probability*

$$\alpha^u(\mathbf{E}, \pi_m) = 1 - \left(\frac{E}{\pi_m}\right)^{\frac{1}{N'-1}}.$$

Upon entering, the firms set their prices according to the mixed strategy distribution

$$F(p) = \frac{1}{1 - \left(\frac{E}{\pi_m}\right)^{\frac{1}{N'-1}}} \left[1 - \left(\frac{E}{pD(p)}\right)^{\frac{1}{N'-1}}\right] \text{ for } p \in [\underline{p}, p_m].$$

Each firm's expected profit, net of entry costs, is zero. The expected price strictly increases in the number of potential entrants, N'.

As is evident from comparing the symmetric and asymmetric cases, even small perturbations away from symmetry lead to dramatically different predictions about the firms' behavior. In the symmetric case, all firms enter with positive probability in the maximal Nash equilibrium. However, once the firms' entry costs differ by even an arbitrarily small amount, then only two firms enter with positive probability, and the firm with the lowest entry cost enters with probability one. The fact that the firm with the lowest entry cost is most likely to enter has more intuitive appeal than the related result in Part (3) of Corollary 1, in which a firm is more likely to enter the higher is its entry cost.

Even though the number of active firms differs once entry costs differ, it is not immediately clear how the expected price changes. After all, the firms' entry probabilities change when only two firms are active, and the change in entry probabilities also changes firms' price-setting behavior upon entering. Fortunately, one can compare the equilibrium price distributions upon introducing any type of asymmetry into the symmetric model. Proposition 3 illustrates one type of asymmetry for which this comparison yields a strong result.

Proposition 3 *Suppose that initially all firms have identical entry cost $E > 0$. If each firm i's entry cost is perturbed by a different amount Δ_i to $E + \Delta_i \geq 0$, with $\Delta_i < 0$ for at least two of the firms, then the expected price strictly decreases.*

Proposition 3 shows that if each firm's entry cost, E, is changed so that at least two of the firms have entry costs strictly less than E, then the expected price falls. The expected price falls further for additional reductions in the two lowest entry costs.

LR show that the expected price is lowest when there are only two potential entrants, under the assumption that all potential entrants have the same entry cost. Consequently, if the entry costs in the duopoly setting are perturbed in the manner described in Proposition 3, so that $E_1 < E_2 < E$, then the expected price falls further. With the introduction of mean zero random shocks to all firms' entry costs in the symmetric model, it is quite likely that the entry costs for at least two of the firms will fall. Therefore, if initially there exist $N' \geq 2$ potential entrants with identical entry costs, then introducing differences in those costs frequently causes the expected price to fall.

One also can draw conclusions about the effect on the equilibrium price distribution of the introduction of potential entrants, in the same manner as was done in LR.

Proposition 4 *Suppose that all firms have different entry costs. The introduction of a potential entrant strictly decreases the expected price if and only if the entrant has the lowest or second lowest entry cost.*

Introducing a potential entrant that has the third lowest entry cost, or higher, has no effect on any firm's entry probability. If the new potential entrant has the lowest or the second lowest entry cost, then its introduction leads to more frequent entry and to more aggressive price-setting upon entering. One can show that the expected price increases if and only if the new potential entrant has the same entry cost as the firm initially with the second lowest entry cost. Consequently, in the asymmetric model, introducing a potential entrant typically does not increase the expected price, in sharp contrast to the symmetric model.

4 Conclusion

This paper analyzes a two-stage entry and pricing game amongst producers of homogeneous products. By permitting firms to have different entry costs, the paper extends the analyses in two recent papers that assume that firms' entry costs are identical. I find that the existing results depend critically on the symmetry assumption.

Elberfeld and Wolfstetter [1999] assume that the firms make their price offers after the number of actual entrants is made known. Their finding that welfare falls as the number of potential entrants increases is not an artifact of the assumption that entry costs are identical across firms. However, in the general model the conclusion is not unambiguous, in contrast to the symmetric model. In the general model, welfare decreases following an increase in the number of firms that enter with positive probability. In the symmetric model, a new potential entrant always can be accommodated by the incumbents without inducing exit. Consequently, expected total welfare strictly decreases in the number of potential entrants in the symmetric model. However, in the general model, welfare strictly increases following the introduction of a potential entrant, provided that the introduction induces the exit of one or more of the original active potential entrants. Exit is induced if the new potential entrant's entry cost is sufficiently low. Thus, introducing the right potential entrants increases welfare, a result which has greater intuitive appeal than the result from the symmetric model.

Lang and Rosenthal [1991] assume that the firms make their price offers without knowing the number of actual entrants. When firms have different entry costs, the equilibrium involves positive entry probabilities only for the two firms with the lowest and second lowest entry costs. In contrast, in the symmetric setting all firms enter with the same positive probability. Thus, changing the symmetric setting by introducing arbitrarily small differences in firms' entry costs leads to vastly different predictions about entry and pricing behavior. Moreover, given that the expected price in the symmetric setting is lowest when potential entry is limited to only two firms, introducing slight differences in potential entrants' entry costs frequently causes the expected price to decrease. Finally, introducing a new potential entrant in the asymmetric setting typically reduces the expected price or has no price effect, in contrast to the unambiguous increase in the expected price found in the symmetric model.

Appendix

Proof of Lemma 1: In equilibrium, firm i's expected payoff, gross of its entry cost, must equal its entry cost. Hence,

$$\left(\prod_{k\neq i}(1-\alpha_k^o)\right)\pi_m = E_i. \tag{1}$$

The same relationship holds for any other firm j, so

$$\left(\prod_{k\neq j}(1-\alpha_k^o)\right)\pi_m = E_j.$$

Taking the ratio of the two preceding expressions yields

$$\frac{1-\alpha_j^o}{1-\alpha_i^o} = \frac{E_i}{E_j}.$$

The preceding relationship can be used in equation (1) to yield

$$(1-\alpha_i^o)^{N-1}\left(\frac{E_i^{N-1}}{\prod_{k\neq i} E_k}\right)\pi_m = E_i. \tag{2}$$

Solving (2) for α_i^o yields

$$\alpha_i^o(\mathbf{E}, \pi_m) = 1 - \frac{\left(\frac{1}{\pi_m}\prod_{k=1}^N E_k\right)^{\frac{1}{N-1}}}{E_i},$$

which is the desired result.

Using the expression for α_i^o, simple algebra yields the expressions for $\rho_b(\boldsymbol{\alpha}^o)$, $\rho_c(\boldsymbol{\alpha}^o)$, and $\rho_m(\boldsymbol{\alpha}^o)$. The expression for total welfare then follows. ■

Proof of Corollary 1: (1) The derivative of $\alpha_i^o(\mathbf{E}, \pi_m)$ with respect to E_i is

$$\frac{d\alpha_i^o(\mathbf{E}, \pi_m)}{dE_i} = \left(\frac{N-2}{N-1}\right)\left(\frac{1}{\pi_m}\prod_{k\neq i} E_k\right)^{\frac{1}{N-1}}\left(E_i^{\frac{3-2N}{N-1}}\right),$$

which is strictly positive for $N > 2$. The derivative is zero is for $N = 2$.

(2) The derivative of $\alpha_i^o(\mathbf{E}, \pi_m)$ with respect to E_j, $j \neq i$, is

$$\frac{d\alpha_i^o(\mathbf{E}, \pi_m)}{dE_j} = -\left(\frac{1}{N-1}\right)\frac{\left(\frac{1}{\pi_m}\prod_{k=1}^N E_k\right)^{\frac{1}{N-1}}}{E_iE_j},$$

which is strictly negative.

(3) Follows from simple algebra.

(4) The derivative of $\rho_b(\boldsymbol{\alpha}^o)$ with respect to E_i is

$$\frac{d\rho_b(\boldsymbol{\alpha}^o)}{dE_i} = \left(\frac{1}{N-1}\right)\frac{\left(\frac{1}{\pi_m}\right)^{\frac{N}{N-1}}\left(\prod_{k=1}^N E_k\right)^{\frac{1}{N-1}}}{E_i},$$

which is strictly positive.

(5) The derivative of $W^o(\boldsymbol{\alpha}^o, \mathbf{E}, \pi_m)$ with respect to E_i is

$$\begin{aligned}\frac{dW^o(\boldsymbol{\alpha}^o, \mathbf{E}, \pi_m)}{dE_i} &= \frac{1}{\pi_m}\left[1 - \left(\frac{N}{N-1}\right)\frac{\left(\frac{1}{\pi_m}\prod_{k=1}^N E_k\right)^{\frac{1}{N-1}}}{E_i}\right] CS_m + \\ &\quad \frac{1}{\pi_m}\left[\frac{\left(\frac{1}{\pi_m}\prod_{k=1}^N E_k\right)^{\frac{1}{N-1}}}{E_i} - 1\right] CS_c.\end{aligned}$$

Premultiplying by π_m and using the expression for $\alpha_i^o(\mathbf{E}, \pi_m)$ yields

$$\pi_m\left(\frac{dW^o(\boldsymbol{\alpha}^o, \mathbf{E}, \pi_m)}{dE_i}\right) = \left[1 - \left(\frac{N}{N-1}\right)(1-\alpha_i^o)\right] CS_m - [\alpha_i^o] CS_c < \alpha_i^o [CS_m - CS_c] < 0,$$

which gives the desired result. ■

Proof of Proposition 1: Suppose the introduction of a new potential entrant induces exit. The number of firms in the maximal Nash equilibrium remains at N, but one participating firm's entry cost has been reduced. By Part (4) of the Corollary, the probability of market breakdown strictly decreases.

Suppose the introduction of a new potential entrant does not induce exit. There are two cases to consider. First, suppose that there are still N firms in the maximal Nash equilibrium, but that $E_e > E_N$. In that case, the behavior of the N firms in the maximal Nash equilibrium of interest is unchanged from their behavior before the introduction of the potential entrant. Consequently, the probability of market breakdown is unchanged.

Second, suppose that there are $N+1$ firms in the maximal Nash equilibrium. Consider the lowest possible entry cost for the new potential entrant that does not induce exit, namely

$$E_e = \left(\frac{1}{\pi_m}\prod_{k=1}^N E_k\right)^{\frac{1}{N-1}}.$$

If E_e is any less, then exit will be induced. With the preceding entry cost, in the new maximal Nash equilibrium the new potential entrant enters with probability zero, and the original N firms enter with the same probability with which they entered in the initial maximal Nash equilibrium. Thus, the probability of market breakdown in the maximal Nash equilibrium with $N+1$ firms is the same as in the maximal Nash equilibrium with N firms. As E_e increases, the probability of market breakdown strictly increases, by Part (4) of the Corollary. Thus, if exit is not induced, then the probability of market breakdown weakly increases. ■

Proof of Proposition 2: Suppose the introduction of a new potential entrant induces exit. The number of firms in the maximal Nash equilibrium remains at N, but one firm's entry cost has been reduced. By Part (5) of the Corollary, expected total welfare strictly increases.

Suppose the introduction of a new potential entrant does not induce exit. There are two cases to consider. First, suppose that there are still N firms in the maximal Nash equilibrium, but that $E_e > E_N$. In that case, the behavior of the N firms in the maximal Nash equilibrium of interest is unchanged from their behavior before the introduction of the potential entrant. Consequently, expected total welfare is unchanged.

Second, suppose that there are $N + 1$ firms in the maximal Nash equilibrium. Consider the lowest possible entry cost for the new potential entrant that does not induce exit, namely

$$E_e = \left(\frac{1}{\pi_m} \prod_{k=1}^{N} E_k \right)^{\frac{1}{N-1}} .$$

If E_e is any less, then exit will be induced. With the preceding entry cost, in the new maximal Nash equilibrium the new potential entrant enters with probability zero, and the original N firms enter with the same probability with which they entered the initial maximal Nash equilibrium. Thus, expected total welfare in the maximal Nash equilibrium with $N + 1$ firms is the same as in the maximal Nash equilibrium with N firms. As E_e increases, expected total welfare strictly decreases, by Part (5) of the Corollary. Thus, if exit is not induced, then expected total welfare weakly decreases. ■

Proof of Lemma 2: Suppose each firm i enters with probability α_i^u. Map each α_i^u into a β_j ordered such that $\beta_1 \geq \beta_2 \geq \cdots \geq \beta_{N'}$, and let $\boldsymbol{\beta} \equiv \{\beta_1, \beta_2, \ldots, \beta_{N'}\}$. I first show there are no pure strategy equilibria. Suppose each entering firm i sets price p_i with probability one. No firm sets a price less than $\left(\prod_{k \neq i} (1 - \beta_k)\right) \pi_m$, as firm i can guarantee itself that expected profit by setting price p_m. Thus, the minimum price set is strictly greater than zero. At least one firm sets the minimum price. If no other firm sets the minimum price, then the firm setting the minimum price has an incentive to raise its price to be arbitrarily close to the next highest price of the other firms. If at least one other firm sets the minimum price, then a firm setting the minimum price has an incentive to undercut that price slightly. Thus, there can be no pure strategy equilibria. For the same reasons, there be no mass points on any price strictly less than p_m, and at most one firm can set price p_m with positive probability.

Given that entering firms use a mixed strategy in equilibrium, I now show that the supports of all entering firms' mixed strategy distributions have the same minimum. Suppose firms i and j have different lower supports for their mixed strategy distributions, with firm i setting the minimum price, so that $\underline{p} = \underline{p}_i < \underline{p}_j$. Price $\underline{p_i}$ wins with probability one, while price $\underline{p_j}$ wins with probability less than one.

Denote firm i's **interim expected profit** when it sets price p and firms enter with the probabilities in $\boldsymbol{\beta}$ by $\pi_i(p|\boldsymbol{\beta})$. Now $\pi_i\left(\underline{p}_i|\boldsymbol{\beta}\right) = \pi_j\left(\underline{p}_i|\boldsymbol{\beta}\right)$. Also,

$$\pi_i\left(\underline{p}_j|\boldsymbol{\beta}\right) = \prod_{k\neq i}\left[1 - \beta_k F_k\left(\underline{p}_j\right)\right]\left(\underline{p}_j - c_L\right)$$

and

$$\pi_j\left(\underline{p}_j|\boldsymbol{\beta}\right) = \prod_{k\neq j}\left[1 - \beta_k F_k\left(\underline{p}_j\right)\right]\left(\underline{p}_j - c_L\right),$$

where $F_k(p)$ denotes the mixed strategy price distribution employed by firm k. Comparing the two, it is evident that

$$\pi_i\left(\underline{p}_j|\boldsymbol{\beta}\right) > \pi_j\left(\underline{p}_j|\boldsymbol{\beta}\right).$$

Now

$$\pi_i\left(\underline{p}_i|\boldsymbol{\beta}\right) \geq \pi_i\left(\underline{p}_j|\boldsymbol{\beta}\right) > \pi_j\left(\underline{p}_j|\boldsymbol{\beta}\right).$$

However, $\pi_i\left(\underline{p}_i|\boldsymbol{\beta}\right) = \pi_j\left(\underline{p}_i|\boldsymbol{\beta}\right)$, which implies $\pi_j\left(\underline{p}_i|\boldsymbol{\beta}\right) > \pi_j\left(\underline{p}_j|\boldsymbol{\beta}\right)$, which violates the equilibrium requirement $\pi_j\left(\underline{p}_j|\boldsymbol{\beta}\right) \geq \pi_j\left(\underline{p}_i|\boldsymbol{\beta}\right)$. Consequently, the supports of all entering firms' mixed strategy pricing distributions have the same minimum. As the minimum price in the support wins with probability one, then each firm has the same expected payoff, gross of entry costs, upon entering. Reverting to the ranking by α_i^u rather than by β_i, denote that expected profit by $\pi(\boldsymbol{\alpha}^u)$.

Suppose that in equilibrium firm $j \geq 3$ enters with positive probability. For firm j to enter, it must be that $\pi(\boldsymbol{\alpha}^u) \geq E_j$. Consequently, $\pi(\boldsymbol{\alpha}^u) > E_2 > E_1$, which implies that firm 1 and firm 2 each enter with probability one. Such entry behavior by firm 1 and firm 2 implies that $\pi(\boldsymbol{\alpha}^u) = 0$, which in turn contradicts $\pi(\boldsymbol{\alpha}^u) \geq E_j$. Therefore, no firm $j \geq 3$ enters with positive probability.

If in equilibrium only firm 1 enters with positive probability, then it will set a price of p_m upon entering. In this case, any other firm will enter with probability one and slightly undercut firm 1, thus upsetting the purported equilibrium. Consequently, it cannot be the case that only firm 1 enters with positive probability. By similar reasoning, firm 2 cannot be the only firm that enters with positive probability.

If in equilibrium firm 2 enters with positive probability, then it must be the case that $\pi(\boldsymbol{\alpha}^u) \geq E_2$. Consequently, $\pi(\boldsymbol{\alpha}^u) > E_1$, and firm 1 enters with probability one.

I now derive the firms' expected profit upon entering. Firm 1 always can earn an expected profit of $(1-\alpha_2^u)\,\pi_m$ by setting price p_m. Hence, firm 1 will never set a price strictly less than $(1-\alpha_2^u)\,\pi_m$. Moreover, the lowest price in the support of the mixed strategy distributions wins with probability one. Consequently, $\underline{p}$ cannot strictly exceed $(1-\alpha_2^u)\,\pi_m$, or else firm 1 will not receive the same expected profit from all prices in the support of the mixed strategy distribution. Therefore, $\underline{p} = (1-\alpha_2^u)\,\pi_m$. Consequently, each firm's expected profit, upon entering, is $(1-\alpha_2^u)\,\pi_m$. Because firm 2 must be indifferent between entering and not entering, it must be the case that $(1-\alpha_2^u)\,\pi_m = E_2$, which implies that

$$\alpha_2^u(\mathbf{E},\pi_m) = 1 - \frac{E_2}{\pi_m}.$$

Any price p in the support of the mixed strategy distribution must yield an expected profit of $(1-\alpha_2^u)\,\pi_m$. For firm 1, it must be the case that

$$[1-\alpha_2^u(\mathbf{E},\pi_m)\,F_2(p)]\,pD(p) = (1-\alpha_2^u(\mathbf{E},\pi_m))\,\pi_m.$$

Using the previously derived expression for $\alpha_2^u(\mathbf{E},\pi_m)$, one can manipulate the preceding expression to show that

$$F_2(p) = \frac{1}{1-\frac{E_2}{\pi_m}}\left[1-\frac{E_2}{pD(p)}\right] \text{ for } p \in [\underline{p}, p_m].$$

A similar argument establishes that

$$F_1(p) = \begin{cases} 1-\frac{E_2}{pD(p)} & \text{for } p \in [\underline{p}, p_m) \\ 1 & \text{for } p = p_m \end{cases}.$$

Finally, as each firm's expected profit, upon entering, is $(1-\alpha_2^u(\mathbf{E},\pi_m))\,\pi_m$, firm 1's expected profit from the two-stage game is $E_2 - E_1$, while firm 2's expected profit is zero. ■

Proof of Lemma 3: Using the argument in the proof of Lemma 2, suppose that in equilibrium firm $j > k$ enters with positive probability. For firm j to be willing to enter, it must be the case that $\pi(\boldsymbol{\alpha}^u) \geq E_j$. Consequently, $\pi(\boldsymbol{\alpha}^u) > E$, and each of the first k firms enters with probability one, which contradicts $\pi(\boldsymbol{\alpha}^u) \geq E_j$. Therefore, in equilibrium no firms other than the first k enter with positive probability.

Consider an equilibrium in which each of the first k firms enters with the same probability, α^u. Following the argument shown in the proof of Lemma 2, a firm's expected profit upon entering, gross of entry costs, is

$$\pi\left(\boldsymbol{\alpha}^u\right) = \left(1-\alpha^u\right)^{k-1}\pi_m.$$

In equilibrium, the expected payoff from entering must equal the expected payoff from not entering. Hence,

$$\left(1-\alpha^u\right)^{k-1}\pi_m = E,$$

from which one can determine that

$$\alpha^u\left(\mathbf{E},\pi_m\right) = 1-\left(\frac{E}{\pi_m}\right)^{\frac{1}{k-1}}.$$

As a firm's expected profit upon entering, gross of entry costs, must equal $\pi\left(\boldsymbol{\alpha}^u\right)$ for any price p in the support, $[\underline{p}, p_m]$, of the mixed strategy distribution, $F(p)$, it must be the case that

$$\left[1-\alpha^u\left(\mathbf{E},\pi_m\right)F(p)\right]^{k-1} pD(p) = \left(1-\alpha^u\left(\mathbf{E},\pi_m\right)\right)^{k-1}\pi_m.$$

Using the previously derived expression for $\alpha^u\left(\mathbf{E},\pi_m\right)$, one can manipulate the preceding expression to show that

$$F(p) = \frac{1}{1-\left(\frac{E}{\pi_m}\right)^{\frac{1}{k-1}}}\left[1-\left(\frac{E}{pD(p)}\right)^{\frac{1}{k-1}}\right] \quad \text{for } p\in[\underline{p},p_m],$$

which is the desired expression. Finally, each firm's expected profit, upon entering, is

$$\left(1-\alpha^u\left(\mathbf{E},\pi_m\right)\right)^{k-1}\pi_m.$$

Using the expression for $\alpha^u\left(\mathbf{E},\pi_m\right)$, each firm's expected profit from the two-stage game is zero. ■

Proof of Proposition 3: Suppose all firms have entry cost $E>0$. Consider a perturbation to each firm's entry cost so that firms 1 and 2 have entry costs E_1 and E_2 strictly less than E, and such that all other firms' entry costs strictly exceed E_2. The equilibrium entry probabilities and mixed strategy pricing distributions are presented in Lemma 2. The distribution of the winning price is

$$H(p) = 1-\left[1-F_1(p)\right]\left[1-\alpha_2^u\left(\mathbf{E},\pi_m\right)F_2(p)\right].$$

Using the results from Lemma 2, $H(p)$ may be written

$$H(p) = 1 - \left[\frac{E_2}{pD(p)}\right]^2.$$

Let $G_N(p)$ denote the distribution of the winning price in the N-firm symmetric case described by LR, and assume that the "price" charged is p_m in the event that zero firms enter. Using Result 2, one can show

$$G_2(p) = 1 - \left[\frac{E}{pD(p)}\right]^2.$$

LR shows that $G_N(p)$ is largest for $N = 2$, which implies that the expected price is lowest when $N = 2$. Note that $H(p) \geq G_2(p)$, with strict inequality for some p, which implies that the expected price is strictly lower with $E_1 < E_2 < E$ than with $N \geq 2$ firms each with entry cost E. ■

Proof of Proposition 4: Suppose that $E_e < E_1$. Denote the equilibrium mixed strategy pricing distributions by $\widetilde{F}_e(p)$ and $\widetilde{F}_1(p)$, respectively. Denote the distribution of the winning price in the new equilibrium by

$$\widetilde{H}(p) = 1 - \left[1 - \widetilde{F}_e(p)\right]\left[1 - \widetilde{\alpha}_1^u(\mathbf{E}, \pi_m)\widetilde{F}_1(p)\right],$$

where $\widetilde{\alpha}_1^u(\mathbf{E}, \pi_m)$ is firm 1's entry probability in the new equilibrium. Using Lemma 2, one can write

$$\widetilde{H}(p) = 1 - \left[\frac{E_1}{pD(p)}\right]^2.$$

Recalling the distribution of the winning price in the original equilibrium, calculated in the proof of Proposition 3 and denoted $H(p)$, one can show easily that $\widetilde{H}(p) \geq H(p)$, with strict inequality for some p. Consequently, the expected price is strictly lower in the new equilibrium.

A similar argument holds when $E_1 < E_e < E_2$. In the remaining case, when $E_2 < E_e$, the introduction of a new potential entrant does not change firms' equilibrium behavior or the expected price. ■

References

[1] Elberfeld, W., and Wolfstetter, E. "A Dynamic Model of Bertrand Competition with Entry." *International Journal of Industrial Organization*, Vol. 17 (1999), pp. 513-525.

[2] Janssen, M., and Rasmusen, E. "Bertrand Competition Under Uncertainty." unpublished manuscript (1999).

[3] Lang, K., and Rosenthal, R. "The Contractors' Game." *RAND Journal of Economics*, Vol. 22, No. 3 (1991), pp. 329-338.

[4] Levin, D., and Smith, J. "Equilibrium in Auctions with Entry." *The American Economic Review*, Vol. 84, No. 3 (1994), pp. 585-599.

[5] Sharkey, W., and Sibley, D. "A Bertrand Model of Pricing and Entry." *Economics Letters*, Vol. 41 (1993), pp. 199-206.

[6] Thomas, C. "The Competitive Effect of Mergers Between Asymmetric Firms." Federal Trade Commission Working Paper # 220 (1998).

www.ingramcontent.com/pod-product-compliance
Lightning Source LLC
Chambersburg PA
CBHW081320180526
45170CB00007B/2786
* 9 7 8 1 5 2 3 3 2 6 5 8 7 *